One Act Play

I0201094

# The will

**An original work**

**By**

*Charlie Navi*

## "Dedicated to Michael Jackson"

Your immense talent set a line to reach, breaking barriers,

Encouraging me to innovate and be unique, a show stopper, nothing more,

Then your true humanitarian being set a heart to reach, those in need,

The one and only King of Pop!

**Plot:** A confused man meets a young soul, falls in love, but fails on his role in society.


**Set:** Small town named Millians in northern California, U.S.A. 2004.


## CHARACTERS


**Amy Holloway:** 18 years old, college pupil, naïve.


**Mrs. Holloway:** Amy's mother, elitist, and wealthy.


**Robert:** 30 years old, priest, insecure.


**Taylor smith:** Amy's confidante, extroverted.


**Mrs. Robinson:** obsessed devotee, conceited.

**Devotee:** mid aged, nosy.

**Mr. Wilhem:** 50 years old, Robert's step-father, wise, and blunt.

**Cashier:** young and amicable.

**Acquaintance:** Hispanic, early twenties.

**Student:** Caucasian, early twenties.

# Scene I

*Robert enters a crowded coffee shop*

Cashier: hi sir what would you like to order?

Robert: mmm... a vanilla one please.

Cashier: ok what size?

Robert: small one (looks over for a place to sit, waits 5 minutes).

Cashier: here you go sir, enjoy it!

Robert: (pays and he walks towards the couch and sits)

Amy: (walks in abruptly with Taylor, both laughing) yes it was hilarious, haha, anyhow, let's sit over there (next to Robert).

Taylor: (they both sit) ok guess what, I'll read, you write!

Amy: is that so! (giggles) ok, (takes a notebook and pen out of her backpack)

Taylor: (takes a book out of her backpack) ok mmm... we were on page twenty four, love this part, ready?

Amy: yeah!

Taylor: and then he says " If the stars were to fall then God would be mad and I'd be in delight, your eyes are my light, cannot deny, but you are so far from my soul, up in the sky, just like a star that shines in my heart".

Robert: (overhears, thrilled by the line) quiet a good line, is simply phenomenal!

Taylor: mmm... yes, well remarkable, have you read the book?

Robert: (shows his book) I am, pardon me I... I am Robert (extends his trembling hand).

Taylor: alright, nice to meet you I'm Taylor and she is Amy.

Amy: hi!

Robert: so what do you study for?

Taylor: Literature II.

Robert: what is your favorite part from the book mmm... Amy?

Amy: ah! well don't laugh, but so far *The Forbidden Garden*.

Robert: oh really, what a coincidence, mine too.

*An hour passes by, the three of them are outside the coffee shop, Taylor says good bye to Robert and Amy, they start walking the opposite direction, while smoking, Amy and Robert exchange numbers*

Mrs. Robinson: (walks by) good evening Robert (stares at Amy) dear.

Robert and Amy: good evening (they wait until she is far and continue talking)

Robert: where do you know her from?

Amy: mmm... she is my mom's friend, where do you know her from?

Robert: me, mmm... actually I don't, she just seemed familiar to me. I believe she is a very devoted citizen, goes to mass all days, however I've heard she is talkative you know! you shouldn't trust her.

Amy: get it.

*Light fades slowly as they exit the stage*

# Scene II

Taylor: (walks towards a bench and sits) shoot why my mom can't be a normal person! (lies down) and be late to any appointment!

Amy: (enters stage right behind Taylor) hi, what are you nagging about?

Taylor: well my mom dropped me an hour early, because she has to run her stupid errands, and has an appointment, God knows where.

Amy: relax; nobody has died for waking up early.

Taylor: no, then is the preamble to it.

Amy: besides you are always, on time for your appointments (sarcastically).

Taylor: shut up (stands suddenly) and speaking of such, how'd it go with Mr. Freako?

Amy: he is not a freako (laughs).

Taylor: (playfully) oh so now you defend him huh!

Amy: no, is just... simply a nice individual (looks at her watch).

Taylor: individual! what the heck (mockingly asks) did Mr. Individual coerce you to visit the forbidden garden?

Amy: mmm… no, we just talked, exchange numbers and so, you know.

*A student passes by, and Amy looks at her watch again*

Taylor: do we have anything for today?

Amy: hello, world history, fascism!

Taylor: crap let's go, puttana! (out- loud, as they exit the stage, in a rush).

Amy: what, hey wait (goes after Taylor).

*Light fades slowly*

# Scene III

*Robert enters stage dressed as a priest, ponders in front of a Christ figure, then kneels*

Robert: is being distracted of my duties a failure or a sign? God please guide me, I cannot concentrate on your word or understand it lately. I know is preposterous, believe me I know, but... why is our nature prohibited and condemned, when expressed openly? You know sometimes I cogitate, if you my lord being omnipotent do not choose to restrain us from walking the tempting trail of feelings. My heart had been idle for many years, without killing me, beating up for thirty years, and my soul being deaf to hear it. Such dichotomy imperils the now uncertain quest of mine, here on earth. However I feel free and compelled to confess before thee, I am jaunty and frustrated, but utterly determined to fulfill your will my lord, you know the reason.

Mr. Wilhem: (enters stage from opposite side, holding a jacket) insanity perhaps

Robert: Mr. Wilhem I...

Mr. Wilhem: is not me you have to worry son, but yourself. Sometimes our reality is insanity to others, and our joviality their sadness. Has it ever happened to you, when you write a letter, the one who reads it, gets back to you, with "what do you mean"

Robert: (stands and walks towards Mr. Wilhem) mmm... yes.

Mr. Wilhem: well that is merely, because you write from your perspective, your standpoint, the way you see the world. You ought to walk others' space, dissect their background and idiosyncrasy, in order to see the real truth, but that my friend, is not what Millians community will get to see from you (he takes a flask and drinks) they will only see the mud before their biased eyes.

Robert: you are right, God, all the ignorance seems to be ingrained, before anything else. You know Mr. Wilhem all these years I've tried to fulfill someone else's expectations and desires, instead of mine. I see the magic in the pictures of my youth, but missed it. I have followed the stream, I have obeyed not lived. From the beginning I was taught the only love to find was God's, if I wanted to do something of my choice would not be allowed, and simply pointed out as wrong. Simple things, like going to the circus, looking for bats in the caves, reading about them, and so many other things.

Mr. Wilhem: (mocking) I picture your mother "Robert come here, those are nature's rejects, the very same devil's creatures". Your mother is a unique character, I love her very much. You know deep inside she is one of the most tender women, I have ever known, but Robert do not do, what you hate the most; there is no school to be a parent.

Robert: so you truly believe, people must persevere on what gives sense to their lives, even though it might... give the sense of sadness to others?

Mr.Wilhem: absolutely yes, as long as it doesn't stop them from living.

Robert: (looks down and ponders).

Mr. Wilhem: look son, whatever you have on mind must be accomplished; otherwise you will live unhappy ever after. But make sure you have measured every angle of it.

Robert: my mind is about to burst, regarding this new course my life will take, after the release, would be like learning how to babble, how to walk, simply how to live. I must tell you Mr. Wilhem the right and wrong, is a very irksome matter to me; society is so obstinated with it, when in the past, people judged any action I did, would get so upset, and frustrated, because I could not retaliate. Simply because this role confines me to always be kind, I wonder why people are so judgmental, and live off of others lives.

Mr. Wilhem: well...

Robert: they speak for what their mind makes, without examining, forgetting the reason; they scrutinize, and not stop by their possible dreadful deeds and past. Is not about illiteracy I am pointing, but rather the malicious nature (looks at the audience) man is bad by nature.

Mr. Wilhem: Robert are you listening to yourself!

Robert: why can't I just leave this (overwhelmed) place to be ...Robert?

Mr. Wilhem: is not that easy son, think of it as the fact that problems and hurdles bring us happiness, if we wouldn't have any, life would be mundane; besides jauntiness is not ever lasting.

Robert: could be.

Mr. Wilhem: it is.

Robert: is unacceptable to me that this community could crucify and vilify without any ground, as if nature was a choice, I am afraid. Look at all the chaos in Iraq, many deaths and not a single weapon of mass destruction found;  How come Bush could be so damned, even at that level, to forget that proof makes the fact.

Mr. Wilhem: Robert there is only one thought to it, bigotry is ignorance (lights a cigarette and offers one to Robert).

Robert: no thank you, have you ever felt or been judged?

Mr. Wilhem: (drinks) yes, more than once, to be precise twenty three years ago, I was working for the government as a school district counselor on the South. Advising teachers how to treat pupils, coming from dysfunctional families, they tend to be hostile, absent, bullied, experiencing drug use as an alternative to their hardships, unwanted pregnancy, you name it. One afternoon as I was leaving my office, I heard someone crying on the adjacent hall, caught my attention and found a young girl, Emily Castellanos; she was an eighteen years old senior at Fillmore High School, a marijuana consumer, pregnant, whose mother had just passed away from a cocaine overdose. I asked her about her plight, and then I was very sorry to hear that her only relative left, was her grandmother. But she could not take care of Emily because she was at a care center for the elderly, so I took the perhaps not so ethic decision of letting her stay at my apartment. Long story short, over the course of two months, the affection increased mutually, and neither Emily nor me denied the connection, but rather acknowledged it. I loved her baby as if it was my son, and dedicated myself to make her happy, to nurture the oasis we both created. She rehabilitated from her addiction, and that is not an easy thing to do; anyhow this dream came to an end, when I shared my story with a colleague from another district. People began to stare at me on the street, as I enquired with close friends, realized they had framed me as someone who took advantage of a vulnerable female, some protests aroused, and I was

fired. Then she ran away, due to the bullying, I was deva -
stated Robert. I could not believe what was happening to me,
and all due to prejudice. Over the next six months had to deal
and overcome a huge depression, and up to these days, do
not know how I was able to continue with my life. My first
thoughts were full of rage, but then felt better knowing it was
the most bona- fide relationship I ever had, and the story
ended up with her death a year later, in a car accident, drunk
driving you know.

Robert: (in shock) I... it's amazing how we turn the world into
chaos, instead of encouraging harmony.

Mr.Wilhem: I know, so will you tell me what is going on, in
that head of yours that will make people frown?

Robert: (looks at Mr. Wilhem in the eyes) is not what is in my
head that matters, but rather defusing the ticking bomb in my
chest (bells tolling, announcing mass, Robert exits stage).

Mr. Wilhem: (confused, then makes a surprise gesture).


*Light fades*

# Scene IV

Amy: (enters from left center, humming a song and carrying an empty basket, as soon as she is off stage back drape opens).

Robert: (on a bench at park, reading a newspaper).

Acquaintance: (passes by, walking a dog) Good morning Father!

Robert: Good morning!


*Half an hour later*


Amy: (walks back, with a full basket)

Robert: Holloway!

Amy: hey, how are you?

Robert: good, here reading the news, relaxing (smiles) how about you?

Amy: well helping my mom with the groceries, so you hang out here... often?

Robert: yes, quite often, is a pleasant environment, would you like to join me?

Amy: mmm... sure, just a moment though.

Robert: may I ? (takes the basket and places it on the ground, as both sit).

Amy: so how is work? Do you have many students?

Robert: students (hesitant) yes of course, about nineteen, is hard memorizing their names you know (smiles).

Amy: well I didn't ask any names (giggles)

Robert: exactly, I love teaching you know, so have you decided what you will major on, after these two years?

Amy: not yet, I might choose something within the medical field, I like taking care of the elderly. Maybe in another city, to take a break from mom, she is so overprotective.

Robert: I am familiar to that; my mother is overprotective, even at this stage of my life. Even though I am independent, still simultaneously smothered by the milieu, at work and personally.

Amy: what's that?

Robert: mmm... the environment, conceited judgmental old people (he stares at her and smiles).

Amy: mom's always worried about being approved by others, silly crap (giggles) so what else do you do? got a girl? Why do you tuck your shirt like that?

Robert: I help at church you know, I do not have a girl, and tuck my shirt because (hesitates) truly don't know (laughs).

Amy: what's her name?

Robert: really don't have anyone at the moment, but I think of someone I like quite often, she is nice and looks very much like you.

Amy: and what's stopping you from acting?

Robert: I... I guess she is terra incognita to me

Amy: what!

Robert: I mean she is the unknown land to me, I do not know how she might react, if I imply ... so do you have a boy in your life?

Amy: used to, but is a family friend, so total boredom; is not like I am a total rebel, but want something different, from another area perhaps, simply a new experience.

Robert: I see.

Amy: nice talking to you, I must go now (grabs the basket) oh untuck your shirt; she might notices you, bye!

Robert: bye (waves his hand) take... care (looks at his shirt) what is wrong with it (untucks his shirt, and continues reading).

*Drape closes*

# Scene V

Mrs. Holloway: (right center, at a kitchen, speaking on the telephone) darling you know how things can go wrong with teenagers, if you become to indulgent (listens) aha Jenin, being worried about Erina's behavior at this moment is understandable, but don't sit on it; let her breathe, be her friend, her confidante, and then little by little she will open up, so you can guide her into the religion and assure her future with a nice, honorable man. Make sure not a single animal is nearby, especially now that nature has taken her shield; otherwise her future would be compromised, yes I am talking about the ... (listens) aha.

Amy: (enters left center stage) I am back mom.

Mrs. Holloway: look Jenin I have to go, my immaculate blessing is here, helping me out in the kitchen (listens) alright, say hi to Milton (listens) ok bye bye.

Amy: here are the groceries mom.

Mrs. Holloway: thank you princess (caresses Amy's hair) come here darling (walks towards the living room and sit on the couch).

Amy: what (follows her) what is going on mom?

Mrs. Holloway: nothing darling, is just that as you grow, I feel we have fallen apart, we should trust each other; be friends not just live here together.

Amy: okay.

Mrs. Holloway: so tell me how things are going in school?

Amy: good we just finished the first quarter tests; I'd say five out of six is an acceptable result.

Mrs. Holloway: six! how come, are you telling me you failed one Amy Holloway?

Amy: relax, not failing, but barely passing (smiles) see mom, History is really boring I try though, but world history is not my thing; I get lost, can't concentrate, I am there physically, but mentally thousand miles away... were you good at this class?

Mrs. Holloway: well good enough to pass and complete my studies, and what do you think when you are thousand miles away, I wonder?

Amy: haha! well things you know, and lately who.

Mrs. Holloway: who! young lady, I am listening.

Amy: mom please don't get upset, is a natural course of life.

Mrs. Holloway: (takes a deep breath) alright, where did you meet this boy?

Amy: at a coffee shop, while doing homework, with Tay... simple coincidence.

Mrs. Holloway: ok does he come from a good family? What is his last name?

Amy: don't push it, you don't know him, he is way different and interesting. The way he talks, and behaves  (she sighs).

Mrs. Holloway: is he from your school?

Amy: no way! I'm over those stuck up dummies

Mrs. Holloway: seriously Amy, you cannot be so gullible just because, they are different and dazzling; see boys will tell you, they are genuinely in love with you, but most of the time, they are only carnal animals. Looking for fun, and taking advantage of girls' feelings, then discard them as if nothing ever happened.

Amy: You mean sex!

Mrs. Holloway: togetherness honey, togetherness!

Amy: whatever.

Mrs. Holloway: I tell you this, because I love you, and must ensure your future, you ought to be my flawless little princess; you will have a family and an honorable husband to cherish.

Amy: look mom I just want to be happy, get the goosebumps whenever I see him. Come on don't you remember, when you fell in love with dad?

Mrs. Holloway: yes (sighs) it was a fairy tale, good gentleman, honorable family, but I took care of myself to avoid compromising my future, therefore as your mother, must take care of yours, keep you on the right path.

Amy: mom I know what I do.

Mrs. Holloway: so how does he look like? tell me.

Amy: alright, he is slender, quiet, and his voice is clear, though he looks old fashioned.

Mrs. Holloway: how so?

Amy: well his hairstyle you know, combed to the left (giggles).

Mrs. Holloway: okay, and what grade is he in?

Amy: mmm... see, he doesn't study anymore.

Mrs. Holloway: (worried) For God's sake, what are you saying, was he expelled?

Amy: no that is why I told you he is different, he does not go to college; he... he teaches philosophy.

Mrs. Holloway: teaches! honey listen to what you are saying, this is utterly unacceptable.

Amy: unacceptable! for your information he already completed his studies, helps at church, works (upset, walks away).

Mrs. Holloway: don't you dare to walk away, while I am still talking (screams) what is his name?

Amy: (stops, faces her mom) don't rush it okay! everything at its time, gosh really thought you wanted to be my friend (exits stage).

Mrs. Holloway: God please guide her (lights up a cigarette) what is his name... (phone rings) hello, hello (hangs up, and sits on the couch).

Amy and Robert: (*a flashing/strobe light reveals both kissing and lewdly caressing each other, all the way backstage*).

*Drape Closes*

## Scene VI

*Few weeks pass by*

Amy: (*she enters stage looks herself in the mirror, then sits on the bed and ponders*).

Mrs. Holloway: (knocks off stage) Amy please let me in!

Amy: go away, I want to be alone!

Mrs. Holloway: honey!

Amy: please! (waits a moment and calls Taylor) hello may I speak to Taylor... thanks ( waits) hey you bimbo! (giggles) hey let's hang out, come to my house (listens) come on! ok see you then (hangs up and takes a notebook and then dials a number) mmm... hello is Robert there? oh hey sorry, I know you told me not to call, during the day. But I feel guilty (listens) don't know, like tramp, I mean. It was only a week and...you were the first (listens) what! I thought you would notice, so at what time is your next class? Ok, hey wait...I love you.

*Light fades and a clock displays twenty minutes later*

Taylor: (knocks) Amy open up!

Amy: hey, why are you sweating?

Taylor: I had to literally run for my life, I was crossing Willow Park, and a stupid german shepherd chased me up.

Amy: hahaha I think I know which one, relax.

Taylor: (takes a deep breath) oh well, so what is on your mind! what do you wanna talk about?

Amy: (sits on the bed) mmm... I already, shoot!

Taylor: already what! no way! who popped the cherry? (laughs) come on tell me!

Amy: hush!! please is not funny, I feel awful.

Taylor: okay sorry, tell me then, when?

Amy: six weeks ago.

Taylor: six weeks ago! and you tell me until now, but you don't even have a boyfriend, I mean, who is it?

Amy: (she stares at her) Robert.

Taylor: Robert Mr. Freako with the tucked shirt, what the hell! So you are already a couple?

Amy: kind of.

Taylor: kind of?

Amy: well see, we can only see each other couple days a week, because of his work.

Taylor: okay, where does he work at?

Amy: can't tell you.

Taylor: can't tell me! I am your best friend.

Amy: seriously.

Taylor: ok then.

Amy: when you meet someone, how long you think should wait to have sex? I mean with Robert it was only a week, but don't know just happened.

Taylor: well I don't think there's a specific time, but the least time, the more risk you take!

Amy: why more risk? He is very nice, you met him.

Taylor: hello! You don't know where the guy has been, with whom etc. Not just because someone is nice or looks clean outside, means is clean inside; but I'm not here to judge, you guys used condom right?

Amy: well, crap!

Taylor: don't you care about yourself Amy? Jesus Christ!

Amy: he told me never been with someone before.

Taylor: yeah right, and the sun is blue (sarcastically).

Amy: (starts crying).

Taylor: (hugs her) you love him huh.

Amy: yes, I know he is good, I feel it.

Taylor: friend, is not only an unwanted pregnancy you need to prevent, but there are also diseases, just imagine how your mother would react to what you've done.

Amy: shut up, she would kill me.

Taylor: listen to me, from now on if Robert loves you, will not oppose wearing a condom.

Amy: you know I cannot buy those things in town, a lot of people know my mom.

Taylor: (takes two condoms out of her brassiere) here you go.

Amy: what, why do you carry them?

Taylor: you never know ( smiles).

Amy: (sighs) well now, I have to take a pregnancy test, because I really need to make sure, everything is alright.

Taylor: and a pap-smear, you have to do it annually, now that you visit the forbidden garden (smiles).

Amy: shut up!

Taylor: so what exactly have you told your mother about Robert?

Amy: not much, actually I barely told her the other day, she is so nosy and pretended to be my friend, so that I would tell her my private things, crushes etc. But when I said Robert was older than me, she went nuts, and I came to my room. I love my mom, but I hate her overprotection, she simply doesn't realize, I am not a little girl anymore; I wish your mom was mine!

Taylor: well there is no school to be a parent, but it must be bothersome to be treated like a child all the time.

Amy: like on prom night, I chose a nice navy blue dress, and got into an argument with her, because of the cleavage.

Taylor: I guess, she would still believe someone gets pregnant by the Holy Spirit (they both laugh).

Amy: let's get something to eat (they both exit stage).

*Light fades slowly*

# SCENE VII

*Three weeks later, On a Sunday, a clock displays minutes before noon at church*

Devotee: good morning Mrs. Robinson! how have you been? I've heard that you just contributed to father Robert's fundraise for the homeless.

Mrs. Robinson: yes darling, I did, I am very concerned for the children's welfare, and Father Robert, is a very compassionate man.

Devotee: I know, if he wasn't a Father, I'd fall for him, he is so charming (sighs).

Mrs. Robinson: oh darling, for God's sake! What are you saying, even if that was so, I think he'd be more into younger women.

Devotee: how so... am I missing something here?

Mrs. Robinson: well God forbids bad deeds, but I saw him, with this very young lady, they seemed to get along very well. But what intrigued me, is the fact he was smoking.

Devotee: yes I knew as well, he was capable of doing some good deeds (giggles) on the side, not morally accepted.

Mrs. Robinson: what are you talking about? Seems you've gotten further than I, go ahead, I am paying attention!

Devotee: two weeks ago, I saw a young lady buying a pregnancy test, as I was waiting in line to purchase my pills, she was nervous so it caught my attention. Don't get me wrong, but I followed this young lady, you know we never see this in our community.

Mrs. Robinson: (very attentive) go on.

Devotee: she got into the church premises through the rear door, what struck me the most, is that she had the keys. I got out of the car, and went over to the side window, and I witnessed the mutual affection, between Father Robert and her. Although she looked upset, he then tried to mitigate her outburst by holding her hands and then kissed her.

Mrs. Robinson: how does this young sinner look like?

Devotee: brunette, with hazel eyes, long hair.

Mrs. Robinson: ok yes same one, I know who she is, now it all makes sense.

Devotee: who is it? Please tell me.

Mrs. Robinson: she is Holloway's daughter, the one up in 24th Drive, so what else did you see?

Devotee: mmm... I see, well, honorable Holloway huh, we should pay a visit, we cannot accept this behavior, so what do you think?

Mrs. Robinson: we should then

*Light fades, a clock displays three hours later*

Mrs. Holloway: (drinking water, and reacts to doorbell) who is it?

Mrs. Robinson and Devotee: good afternoon dear, this is Mrs. Robinson.

Mrs. Holloway: Robinson?

Mrs. Robinson: I am in the church fundraise team.

Mrs. Holloway: (opens the door) good afternoon, sure come on in, I just donated ten thousand dollars; is there anything else you need my help with?

Mrs. Robinson: in fact we do.

Mrs. Holloway: please sit.

Mrs. Robinson: thank you, see I do not know where to start from, but is related to your daughter.

Mrs. Holloway: (worried) what's the matter with her? Is she okay? don't tell me she has been smoking on the church premises.

Mrs. Robinson: well, I am afraid is something quiet more disturbing, do you know if your daughter has a boyfriend?

Mrs. Holloway: yes, she's told me about it, I do not agree and do not know him, but I know she sees someone, older than her (makes a disapproval gesture).

Mrs. Robinson: do you know what he does for a living?

Mrs. Holloway: well I believe he teaches, yes he does.

Mrs. Robinson: Holloway I'd be blunt, he is a Father, and that is why we are here, we cannot accept such immorality in Millians.

Devotee: (looking all over the place, nervously).

Mrs. Holloway: what immorality, in my family no way. Believe me I will intervene, please tell me. Where does he teach at?

Mrs. Robinson: Holloway he is a Father!

Mrs. Holloway: (stares at both of them, with shame) so he has children then.

Mrs. Robinson: For God's sake, he is a priest! (she turns to devotee) tell her what you saw.

Devotee: I...

Mrs. Holloway: (infuriated, listens attentively).

Mrs. Robinson: (taps devotee with her elbow).

Devotee: I saw a young lady buying a pregnancy test, please don't get me wrong, but I followed her, your daughter. And looked over the church side window, she was first upset and then he ... kissed her, Father Robert, but I swear did not mean to follow.

Mrs. Holloway: (struck by the new, starts trembling).

Mrs. Robinson: as you can see, it is a total shame, as they say nothing is what it seems, perhaps your daughter was meant to be a sin.

Mrs. Holloway: shut up! he is the sin, (screams) why!

Devotee: she might be pregnant you know.

Mrs. Holloway: (slaps devotee).

Mrs. Robinson: stop it Holloway! how dare you!

Mrs. Holloway: he seemed so ethical, so full of the word, mendacious bastard!

Devotee: Amy should move out of Millians, far away.

Mrs. Robinson: agree, must take the sin apart.

*Door opens*

Amy: hi mom, good afternoon all, what is... going on?

Mrs. Holloway: (stares at Amy with disdain) how could you (screams) how!

Mrs. Robinson: she found out about your furtive relationship, with Robert.

Amy: mom, I didn't mean to hurt you, I did not know he was a priest, God knows he's a good man (burst into tears).

Mrs. Robinson: you knew, having your encounters at church, please don't lie.

Amy: It was already too late, mom please I know how this hurts you, but he is leaving the church, he will not be a priest anymore.

Mrs. Robinson and devotee: (they look at each other) what!

Robert: (comes in slowly) good afternoon ladies, Amy!

Amy: they knew.

Mrs. Holloway: ( goes yelling and scolding at Robert) you are the very same devil's creature, you have fooled us, we were cajoled into your treacherous being, we put our trust in you, and you paid us by taking my daughter's innocence, death may fall upon you (slaps him).

Amy: mother stop it, is a good thing all of you are here, Robert hasn't taken anything away from me, but rather fulfilled my soul, with God's love and guidance. Before you go any further, let me tell you obsessed ignorant church people, I love him! isn't that what religions is all about, love.

Mrs. Holloway: (tries to slap Robert again).

Robert: ( holds Mrs. Holloways hand) look Mrs. Holloway, your daughter has been the biggest resurrection of my soul, and you do not have to worry for anything else, because she is free now, that means happiness. Yes she is pregnant as I suppose all of you know, I will marry her, and you may think otherwise, but God will let Amy and I into heaven. While all of you will be going to hell, for your attempt on blocking his will!

Mrs. Holloway: (clenches her fist, and exits stage).

Robert: (looks at Amy in the eyes) what have I done (burst into tears and kneels, caressing Amy's womb) if my happiness is a sin, then what is love? God please tell me!

Amy: you are not a sinner, but rather my savior, my fulfillment; don't you see, my soul used to wink, and now (caresses her womb) you made it blink.

Robert: (stands slowly, and stares at her).

Robert and Amy: (they both kiss).

*Light fades abruptly, along with bells tolling*

# Stage notes

# Stage notes

Contact the author for any stage set up or any other copyright authorization at: charlienavi@hotmail.com


Follow the author on instagram at: charlie_navi_jackson

ISBN: 978-607-00-8869-8

Copyright / Derechos de autor

www.ingramcontent.com/pod-product-compliance
Lightning Source LLC
Chambersburg PA
CBHW021148020426
42331CB00005B/953